THE

CHEAT

SHEET:

The Do's & Don'ts When Dating with a Purpose

Andrew R. Mitchell

Published by Mitchell Publishing and Media LLC

ISBN: 978-0-578-80116-2

Dear Reader,

The goal for this book is to make individuals who are looking to be in a relationships aware of the position they play in making that possible. Additionally, this book aims to highlight the ways in which we may unknowingly place ourselves in toxic situations. This can be due to our lack of knowledge about a potential partner, not paying attention to "red flags," and not taking our time in the dating process. I caused a lot of havoc in my prior relationships while going through my own evolution of self, which compelled me to write this book. This book helped me realize that finding love is all about recognizing your own strengths, weaknesses, and love of self. How can you truly love and flourish in a relationship when you don't know how to love *yourself?*! How can you be fair in a relationship when you don't acknowledge your own faults and weakness? I want people to understand that securing a relationship starts with *you* first.

This book was created for women in mind, due to the grief that men, like myself, have put women through as we search for love and companionship. This book will help individuals who are dating to avoid wasting time on individuals who aren't ready to be in a potential relationship. I was a man who gave open promises of love and commitment to women I knew I had no intentions on being with for the long haul. The only difference is that some individuals are very forthcoming with their intentions and others will drag things along, even when recognizing that they do not want the same thing that their counterpart wants. This book is a guide that will provide tips that may help you to navigate the dating process with more ease, as well as assist you in making better choices while trying to secure a potential love relationship. This guide was written through personal and non-personal dating experiences that highlights the good, bad, and ugly stages of dating. Please, feel free to take advantage of the "Cheat Sheet Notes" in the back of the this book—This is your "Cheat Sheet."

INTRODUCTION

I am not a therapist, nor do I have the credentials of a marriage counselor. However, I am a man that has been in love, who has struggled with temptations and addictions. I'm not a perfect man but a man that was plagued by his own imperfections and uncertainties. These imperfections & uncertainties allowed me to see the positive effects of what love, lust, and companionship can have on one's life. Growth is a part of life, and within it, my personal growth allowed me to examine my dealings in dating as well as relationships. Through my personal experiences, as well as others, I decided to create this guide.

The Cheat Sheet was designed as a guide to assist individuals in the dating process by showing the do's and don'ts of dating. The goal of providing this information is to equip individuals with the tools needed to ultimately secure a relationship. This book will also help you in recognizing that what you want may not be what someone else desires. This book will not teach you how to get married, nor will it teach you how to bed a potential partner quicker. However, this book will help you to make better choices when it comes to dating with the intention to secure a relationship.

CHAPTER 1:

THE RIGHT STATE OF MIND

O ur life's experiences are full of lessons that mold us into who we are and/or who we are meant to be. What I feel to be true is that our struggles in keeping and maintaining relationships are what mentally and physically prepare us for the next step, and ultimately, for who we are meant to be with. We will all go through a few bad apples before we meet that person that truly fulfills us. That person who balances us out. That person who completes your mind, body, and soul. If you take advantage of the dating process, you will learn about your likes, dislikes, and what you are actually looking for in a partner. You may date someone who opens your mind up to life, things that you would never pay attention to, admire, or even take advantage of. You can meet someone who turns you off from dating or wanting companionship, who makes you question who you can trust, or may even make you question your value & worth. In my opinion, it's important to get in the right state of mind before you begin to date and/or become involved with someone. To get in the right state of mind, one needs to know exactly what it is they want or need from a potential partner and making it their standard.

When I speak to a lot of women, the number one thing mentioned is the fact that they are tired of dating. They ask themselves

4

why they keep meeting the same type of men. They strongly feel that what all men want to do is have sex. In the beginning, it starts out fine, but in the end, instead of gaining a partner in a relationship, you end up gaining another sexual partner. Ladies, determine what your ultimate goal of dating is. Are you looking for companionship, or would you like it to lead to marriage? Most women I have encountered who are frustrated with just dating ultimately wanted more than just companionship. Many years ago, a sex partner was just that. However, the dynamics have changed.

Most men and women who engage in sexual relationships do almost the same things that someone in an actual relationship title does. Now I won't place all the blame on women because, as a man, we ultimately know whether we are into you & if we want whatever is potentially building to go anywhere. Most men can determine this in two to three months tops. The honorable thing to do would be to inform the person you are having dealings with that you don't see things going in the direction they would like. However, most men aren't honorable. Instead most would allow the situation to go as far as it can go with someone consequently getting hurt. So, as a woman, you need to be in the right state of mind, know what you want, and when you see things not going in that direction, keep pushing. Pay attention to red flags when you meet someone and before you become intimate with them. Now I am all for the spontaneity of sex, but you would be surprised how waiting a week or two can reveal something about someone you are seeing that may ultimately change your mind about sleeping with them. People tend to show their true colors within time so take your time. If you are looking for a relationship, the person who you are dating should exhibit the behavior of someone you would feel compatible with. There's nothing wrong with being open-minded in dating someone who may not normally be your preference. It's also important for you to understand your dating behavior. We often confuse compromising, settling, and our personal preferences thinking that that is being open-minded. All three things mentioned are somewhat related in the aspect of dating but should not be confused as they are still different. Settling can be when you know a person isn't for you when the only thing you guys have in common is a child, home, or sexual appetite. You desire more, but you stay for what you feel is the greater good. A compromise may be a case where you are dating a heavy drinker; you love this person but recognize it's a hard addiction to quit. You come to an understanding that only on events and special occasions it would be acceptable for that person to drink. A compromise is basically when two mutual parties come to an understanding. And lastly, personal preference is usually why some people remain single. There's nothing wrong with having preferences, but if your preferences have you dating the same type of individual, that may be a reason why you still single. So I suggest being a little open-minded. A person can be open-minded enough where they aren't settling and compromising their integrity. And open-minded enough where they are not completely disregarding all of their preferences. Some preferences are good and are a large part of who we are. And some preferences can come across as mean and vain. Some people prefer to date older men or women as others prefer to date younger men or women. Some women, in particular, will not date a man shorter or even the same height as them but wonder why they are still single. I'm not saying you should lower your personal preference but just imagine how much you may be missing out on. Only you know how open-minded you are willing to be; my suggestion is not to be to open. The second thing you need to know or ask yourself when being in the right state of mind is, what's an ideal partner for you? A lot of single people only know what they don't want in a partner. It's just as important to know what you want, don't want, and what you need. As for me, an ideal partner would be someone who brings the best out of me and makes me want to be a better person. Someone that challenges my mind as well as teaches me things about myself I didn't even know. So dig deep and ask yourself what's an ideal person for you. The right state of mind is just being clear on what you ultimately want. It's either you are looking for a good time, or you want a relationship that can lead to something more meaningful, like marriage. Only you will know what type of man you want and what type of man that fulfills you.

CHAPTER 2:
PLAY IT SAFE

T o avoid ending up in an undesired situation, you need to get in the right state of mind. You need to know and understand what it is that you actually want. You need to know whether you want to be in a relationship with a direction that may eventually lead towards marriage or whether you want companionship. Playing it safe is making your intentions known from the very beginning. Let's be clear, even though you may make your intentions clear, that person may or may not go for it, but at least you're not wasting your time leading them on. Most people have lost sight of the idea of dating, which should lead to something bigger and more fulfilling. Those that are currently in relationships would agree that when they started out dating their partner, they dated with the intent of it eventually leading to a relationship. Once you are in that relationship, you may want it to eventually lead to marriage. The key thing in playing things safe is not losing touch of wanting more— the idea of wanting to be more than just a fling or just a new sex partner. The sad thing is: that is exactly what happens.

We date, and it ends up becoming comfortable territory. We end up doing all the things with that partner that most people do in relationships; we do it with no committed relationship. To avoid this, you have to set expectations for yourself and establish what it is you actually want. It's when we don't truly know what we want that we fall victim to the bullshit. We should proceed with caution when meeting someone who portrays qualities that we admire, especially when this person fits the criteria of what we want. We have to be clear on what we want and avoid making statements such as "I'm open to a relationship." It's either you want a relationship, or you don't. When it comes to what you want, the direct approach is always the best. You should always align yourself with someone who is on the same page. And you should never compromise and settle for something you know for sure you don't want. Don't allow anyone to waste your time or insult your intelligence, especially when you know what you want. Would you date someone who wasn't sure if they were interested in you? What if they told you they were open to being interested in you? Would you be open to entertaining the thought of being with them? If you asked someone you've been dating for a few years if they could see themselves marrying you, and they told you they weren't sure, would you continue to date them if you were at a point where you wanted to be married? My point is that if a person isn't showing a mutual interest in you, you shouldn't have to put in extra effort in trying to prove that you are a potential partner for them. There's nothing wrong with being open-minded, but you can't be too open-minded when it comes to your heart. Playing it safe is knowing what you want and not entertaining anyone who doesn't. You can't convince someone they should want the same things you want; they need to see that for themselves. So, always be clear with your feelings as you have to protect your heart and understand that your time is valuable.

The key to dating is for it to lead to a successful relationship. For it to lead to a relationship, you should always be direct with your intentions. There is no need for compromise when it comes to what you want because you are entitled to having expectations. You just need to understand that you may not always get what you want. And that doesn't mean that you did anything wrong or that you should compromise your views for the sake of companionship. It just means that you should understand that some people will rise to the occasion; some will portray that they can rise to the occasion, while others just won't. You want to stay away from the pretenders; those are the ones that show potential, who play word games, who pretty much tell you all you want to hear and don't deliver. It's strange writing about these things as I once played all of these games and broke many hearts along the way. Yet, once I became self-aware and discovered that I, too, was doing these things in a relationship and the hurt that I caused, I took some time away from dating to become a better man and potentially a better partner. I learned that understanding your strengths and weaknesses in life can contribute to you becoming a better person. You start to understand how embracing your strengths and weaknesses can help you make better choices with love, and this understanding places you in better positions in relationships. There isn't such a thing as a perfect relationship, but you can have a loving, understanding, and fulfilling relationship. When I sit back and reflect on some of my past relationships and realize the part I played in them not working, I shake my head in frustration because if I had put more effort into them, they might have worked out. If I had been more honest with myself and my previous partners, those relationships might have been more fulfilling. However, I do recognize that those experiences are what made me a better man today. With that being said, ladies and gentlemen, take your time to determine what you truly want in a relationship or if you even want a relationship at all!

Learn your strengths and weaknesses and how to apply your strengths in dating and in being in a relationship. Know your weaknesses and how you can apply them as strengths in dating and relationships. Understand your positive and negative characteristics and how they can affect arguments and disagreements. To highlight everything as a whole, take the time to know *you* and what *you* want before you take the time to get to know someone else and the possible baggage that they may or may not bring. Playing it safe is truly all about paying attention and allowing yourself to avoid unwanted situations. Below I outline some key points as a reminder.

1. Understand your strengths & weaknesses. When understanding your strengths and weaknesses, you are putting yourself in a position where you can't be manipulated. When arguing,

has your partner ever told you how inconsiderate and insensitive you could be? Once you start recognizing your strengths & weaknesses when in certain situations, you can then take a step back, check yourself, and re-evaluate the situation. In doing so, you can stop certain situations from becoming toxic. In dating, you may have a certain way of being close-minded and may, at times, be unwilling to accept criticism. If you recognize yourself as that person, you can avoid that. I once dealt with a woman who I cared for dearly. We would have discussions about everything. I would give her my opinion about certain fashion choices or how I felt that she should handle certain situations at work or with people. I remind you that we were *dating* one another. She would get upset to the point where she didn't want to talk to me, and at times would get very defensive. I had to constantly remind her that my statements always came out of love. It was later revealed that she was so consumed with her insecurities that it wouldn't allow her to see past what I was saying. Had she faced her insecurities, which in her situation may be a weakness, she may have handled our interactions a lot better. When I did realize that the reasons for our arguments after certain conversations were based on her personal insecurities, I took a step back and tried different approaches. I also took the time to understand my weaknesses, one being that I can come across as being insensitive. My insensitivity has been the cause of several arguments in many of my previous relationships. I recognize that it's not always *what* you say but *how* you say it. When you start to accept your weaknesses, you become at one with yourself; it helps you have day-to-day interactions better.

2. Know what you want. Do you want a relationship or companionship? Know the difference between both. When you want a relationship, you have to let that be known, and there's no room for compromise. When you are just open to companionship, as opposed to desiring a relationship, you should recognize that in some ways, you may be settling or compromising if a relationship is what you truly desire. The issue is being fooled into being a companion, which I will discuss in the next chapter: "THE SITUATION." When you know what you want, there is no room for alternatives. For example, one time, I went to a dealership to purchase a vehicle. I knew exactly what I wanted—at that time, it was a smoke-grey Lexus sedan. The dealer didn't have it and tried to sell me a red Honda Accord trade-in. He knew I was in the market for a car and felt I would be willing to compromise because of it, in addition to the car being a lot cheaper than the one I wanted. My point is that when you know what you

want down to: the color, amenities, and model, there's no room for negotiation. You either have what I want, or you *are* what I want. If you aren't, there's no deal and no need to waste any of my time.

CHAPTER 3

THE SITUATION

T he Situation is when two people meet, one with intentions of finding love and the other with no real intentions. It's a *form* of a relationship because they are intimate with one another. Possibly, you engage in dinner dates, travel, and may even have meaningful conversations from time to time; but there is no title or no real direction on where things are or should lead. This is because, at some point, things got comfortable. I know the situation all too well, as, in the past, I have manipulated situations to avoid getting into a serious relationship and having the responsibility of what relationships bring. When you are in a full-fledged relationship, you and that relationship are held to a higher standard. There are things that are expected of you in that relationship. You are expected to be a lover, a friend, have the potential to provide, and be faithful. The advantage of being in a situation is that you aren't held to that standard and aren't obligated to the same ideas of a relationship. If you step out and are intimate with someone other than the person that you are in a situation with, you won't be scrutinized by your partner and not be at risk of possibly losing your partner as you would in a relationship, because you're in a *situation*. That is what's so appealing to most who aren't looking for a relationship because a situation gives you companionship without having to fully commit.

To truly avoid getting into a situation, you should make your intentions very clear and not compromise on them. However, when it comes to what you want when you clearly know what you want, you have to set that standard and let that expectation be known. So, if you want to be in a relationship, there's no room to compromise, and you certainly shouldn't do relationship things with someone who isn't your partner. Five to ten years ago, I didn't feel this way, and that was the selfishness in me, wasting women's time. I knew that most of the women who I was pursuing or involved with at that time in my life I didn't fully desire them. At times, I tried to convince myself otherwise, as most men do. But for the most part, a person knows from the very beginning where they are willing to allow a situation to go.

In most cases, that person may have placed you in category: fling, friend, or potential companion. With all that being said, if you are looking for a *relationship*, beware of the signs of a *situation*. It may be challenging to even recognize the difference, as a situation mirrors what a relationship is. The key thing is that if you have to ask your partner what we are doing with one another, and where is this going, nine times out of ten, you aren't in a relationship. You should never have to ask a partner where this relationship is going because when someone is into you, you would already know. When someone desires you and has plans for you in their life, they will make damn sure you are aware of their intentions. A situation will

16

have you along for a ride you never truly anticipated on going, where a relationship has the ability to lead you into something more meaningful such as marriage. There are some men and women who may not be looking for a relationship but may be open to the possibilities of one, and there's nothing wrong with that. But the problem is when you know what you want, and they are just "open to it." Entertaining someone like that will have you in a situation. The problem in entertaining a situation like that would arise after you decide to become involved with them and allow them to reap all of the benefits of what a relationship offers. They will then become very complacent. Why make someone your girlfriend or boyfriend when you have all the benefits, especially when that person initially stated they were open-minded to being in a relationship and never clearly stated they desired to be in one. In my opinion, you either want to be in a relationship, or you don't.

Ladies and gentlemen, beware of the word: trickery. You either want to be in a relationship, or you don't—bottom line. If you are someone who is looking to be in a relationship, don't waste your time with someone who isn't. The key thing is knowing what you want and recognizing what you are willing to accept. It's important to take accountability in the role you play, be stern when it comes to your wants and needs. Even though in relationships, you should be willing to compromise, while you're in the dating process, you don't have to. So, never concern yourself with pushing someone away while in the early stages of dating them, especially if you do not feel that they are the right person for you. If they are not for you or do not share similar goals in life as you do, the relationship will never work. Below, I outline some key points as a reminder.

1. Make your intentions clear. For example, one would say, "My name is Drew, and I would like to get to know you." I'm letting you know I would like to get to know you. Your next question should be, "Why?" Now, if Drew replies, "I would possibly like to see where things can go," he would automatically be denied. My point is, when you know what you want, you don't have time to play games. Most people already know their intention from the very start. People can only get away with what you allow them to get away with. So hold people accountable for what they do and what they say. Make sure anyone you give your time to is being very clear with what they want from you, and if they aren't, don't be afraid to shut it down.

2. If you are dating someone for more than three months and you're not officially in a relationship, then end whatever it is you have. Most people already know what they want within three months—if they are still figuring it out, figure it out somewhere else. It's either you know or don't. You want to be a person's first choice.

CHAPTER 4

THE DATING GAME

T he dating process is one of the most unpredictable processes known. When you initially meet someone, you don't know if you are meeting their "representative" or just a sincere individual. You don't even know whether they are crazy or deranged. So, I propose this question, "How well do you know someone you are dating or considering to date?" When dating, are you getting a good feel for this person? Are you paying close attention to details and not blinded by what this person only wants you to see? Does this person meet your standards? What are your standards, and are you willing or open to compromising them?

On the other hand, standards have no room for compromise. An example of a standard would be a person who owns a vehicle but chooses only to date people who have their own vehicles, as well. On the other hand, preferences are things that we like and prefer. People tend to compromise in relationships if the compromise isn't too far off from what they would usually prefer. For example, a person may prefer to date older individuals but would consider dating someone their age. At times, we often confuse our preferences with standards. In doing that, you risk losing out on a potential mate.

Some of us treat dating as a game and date for the thrill of meeting new people in addition to being "wined and dined." But most people date to find someone who they feel compatible with. Once we have established that this person is compatible with us and share the same goals as us, we may then decide to enter a monogamous relationship. Now, if you have read carefully thus far, I stated that you "may" decide to enter into a monogamous relationship. I stated that because not all people desire to be with one person. Some people enjoy the thrill of dating and meeting new people, and there is nothing wrong with that. But when I speak of dating, I'm speaking of the concept of it leading to something more meaningful. Dating and meeting new people can be meaningful if that's what you require. But when I speak of "meaningful," I speak of possibly finding your soul mate, finding someone you can marry and share the rest of your life with. Everyone doesn't believe in marriage, and that's fine, but to still find someone who you are truly compatible with and whom you want to spend the rest of your life with, being monogamous, is just as special. In the dating game, it's crucial for one to be honest and let you know if they are dating more than one person. Honesty is always key and helps keep things on an even playing field. It also helps give a person a choice on whether they want to even get involved with another person—especially when sex is involved, as most people don't want to "willingly" or "knowingly" want to share their partner. I often hear from women on how tired they are of dating.

I understand how frustrating it can be to date different people and allow them into your world and personal space. Sex usually comes along with dating. As a single person trying to find love, it can be frustrating dating and giving them your body to learn three months later that they aren't the one for you, and their goals are not the same—then to start the same pattern with another person. That's why I suggest in the dating game, you proceed with caution with anyone you consider dating. It would help if you were always honest with someone you are dating and do not rush anything. In dating, people have a habit of rushing things, such as sex and when to invite a person to your home. When you rush things, you tend to miss out on important details, you overlook the warning signs. Just know: the best things in life are worth waiting for. This means that I will enjoy my life for what it is. I will live my life as if every day is my last, but I will use my best judgment while I do it. Every situation is different. In some situations, you may be able to make hasty decisions, but when it comes to finding a mate or giving your body to someone, proceed with caution. Overall, understand that the dating game is no game at all; it's life, and decisions you make, whether with caution or hasty, can affect your entire life.

The dating game is truly all about knowing what you want. A lot of people act as if they know what they want but usually chase a feeling. If you truly know what you want and how you want it, I can almost guarantee you will see anyone's bullshit a mile away, as it won't align with your true vision. If you set realistic expectations with yourself and for a potential partner that you want, you will be able to weed out the real from the pretenders. Three keys tips may help you to discover what you want in a partner.

1. Pay full attention to the person you are dating, which is not limited to just what they say to you, how they act when they are around you as well as when they aren't around you.

2. Take your time while dating; it's not a race. If he or she isn't willing to wait, they are probably not the right person for you.

3. I mentioned that most people are out chasing a feeling rather than aligning themselves with a potential partner and/or eventually, a husband or wife. It's easy to get a partner but more difficult to find someone who compliments you and fulfills you mentally, physically, and spiritually—especially without compromising some of your expectations. So, take the time and learn your likes and dislikes in dating. Date yourself, if you must. Dating yourself can help you find happiness within yourself: the happiness that is not given to you through companionship, but that truly comes from within. This is important because some people feel that sense of validation or completion only when they are in a relationship. If you find your happiness within yourself, your partner will be an addition to your

life, not a missing piece. When some people break up, they feel lost because their partner was the "missing piece." However, if you truly love yourself and are not afraid of being alone, you will not easily compromise your feelings for the sake of a potential partner.

CHAPTER 5:

THE TEXT MESSENGER

W e are in the age of technology, where life moves so fast. A time where multi-tasking is a must and technology is used to make those tasks easier. Technology has affected our everyday lives from our interactions at work, with our kids, and even with our partners. This is an era where the first thing people do when they wake up in the morning is to check their mobile devices to see the latest news and trends. When was the last time you had a meaningful conversation over the phone and not through a text message? Ask yourself how many days can you go without text messaging? It saddens me to ask these questions even for myself. However, this is the world we live in.

I, like most people, I'm grateful for the contribution that text messaging has made to our society. Have you ever encountered people who like to talk on the phone, but don't have much to say? Do you often feel like you are the one carrying a conversation when speaking? If you have any of these issues, just send a person a text message. Text messages are usually quick and easy and help avoid long, drawn-out conversations. The reality is that we live in a society of convenience, and we have relied solely on text messaging and not on a good conversation over the phone. So, instead of giving someone your full attention over the phone, you can just shoot them a quick text message. The great thing about texting is that you can be at work performing a work task and have a text conversation at the same time. You can also be at home eating and watching TV while text messaging a friend. However, every conversation is not meant to be text messaged; it can lead to some of the biggest arguments due to someone taking your text message the wrong way. The following things should not be text messaged for obvious reasons.

1. JOB RESIGNATION: Resigning through a text message is unprofessional.

2. PREGNANCY: Announcing a pregnancy is impersonal.

3. BREAKUP: Disrespectful and cowardly.

4. CALLING IN SICK: Unprofessional.

5. PROPOSAL: Impersonal.

6. DEBATES /ARGUMENTS: Messy.

The list goes on, but those were just a few that came to mind. I'm not saying that there is something wrong with texting. Some people are better text messengers than they are conversationalists. However, if it's too lengthy a text, a phone call should be made. Text messaging should not be the main means of communicating when dating! I understand that we are in the age of technology where FaceTime, video messages, and social media exist. But, as you are getting to know someone, stick to the basics, and then gradually utilize other sources. Life isn't always black and white; neither is what is written in text messages. So, even though texting is easy and convenient, it can be misinterpreted, like anything else.

CHAPTER 6

THE 6 RULES OF ONLINE DATING

We live in a civilization where we no longer need landline phones, where speaking on the phone is overrated, and text messaging is a way of life. When it came to meeting and possibly hooking up with a male or female, it used to take time, precision, even dedication. You couldn't just log onto a website and have millions of men and women at your disposal. You couldn't type in your preference on what you look for in a mate and allow the computer to narrow your choices down. You had to take the time and execute a plan to meeting and hooking up with someone. Whether you went to church, school, work, clubs, weddings, even funerals—and yes, some people look to hook up at *funerals*. You would need to have a plan and a proper approach in trying to hook up with someone. I am here to tell you that there are rules of online dating.

Rule Number One

When considering online dating, one should first do their research in finding a trustworthy online dating website. If you are looking for love and not just sex, maybe a website like www.freak-meets.com wouldn't be the right place for you. The name of the website can usually be a good indication of what might be in store within this website. Also, utilize the internet; you can Google certain websites and see feedback from different individuals on their experiences with said site. You can also take into account feedback from friends and coworkers if they have explored the online dating scene.

Rule Number Two

When setting up your profile, make sure your profile is very clear, and your wording is short and brief. You should not give away too much about yourself, but enough to strike interest. If a person does decide to respond to your profile and you revealed too much about yourself, there will be less to talk about. In other words, if you put that you are employed, there's no need to have on your profile list exactly what it is you do for a living. We all should be mindful that some people don't have the best intentions. We have some people looking for a meal ticket for someone to take care of them, and to be quite honest, that's what I call a "come-up." When you set your profile up, you want someone who has good intentions, so the fact that you are employed should be good enough initially. If you have children, you should definitely include that because you don't want to be misleading—For some individuals, that may be a deal-breaker as we all have preferences. However, honesty is the best policy when dealing with online dating and gives the person the right to choose. Just to be clear, the few things that I have suggested thus far are for individuals looking to find potential love online. If that isn't you, please disregard the few things that I've stated. Online dating can be what you make it, to be honest. If you are looking for a good time, meaningless sex, or just companionship, you can find that too, and the great thing is: no rules apply to that. But, if you are looking for something a little more serious, you should proceed with caution and be very precise in what you do and how you do it when it comes to online dating.

Rule Number Three:

If you are indeed looking for something meaningful, I suggest you do not post any provocative photos on the internet. A person's way of dressing or lack of dress can indicate a lot to an individual viewing your internet profile, so keep it classy and in good taste. In other words, do not post pictures that you wouldn't want your parents, children, and/or coworkers viewing. Chances are if it is an issue with any of those individuals viewing those photos, then those photos are probably inappropriate and definitely shouldn't be surfing the net. Ladies, men are very visual people, and you will find that they always want to see more. However, fewer photos and properly dressed photos are best. Men, that goes for you also—if you are to be taken seriously, stay away from posting photos displaying money and lack of clothes as that sends the wrong signal. If you and the person meet up and you are comfortable with sending provocative photos, that would be on your terms. I don't suggest it unless you feel very confident, secure, and comfortable with it, but initially keep it simple.

Rule Number Four

When choosing a profile name, chose something simple and non- sexual, "lickitwet" or "hunglong" may not be appropriate names if you are looking to be taken seriously. Perception is key, so if you do have a provocative name, most people will be curious about the story behind it. In some cases, that can be a good thing depending on the actual screen name. However, it's my personal opinion that you should stay away from sexual conversations or any-thing that comes across as sexually suggestive. So, I would suggest a screen name such as "lifesbeauty" compared to a screen name such as "always_ wet." Both screen names can strike a dialogue. Howev-er, one would strike the *right* dialogue.

Rule Number Five

The great thing about technology is that there are apps where you are able to use a dummy and/or duplicate cell number. I person-ally feel you should take your time before giving your phone num-ber out because people have a tendency of showing their true colors within time. So why give a wrong phone number out to someone who may be a potential dud regardless of the number being legiti-mate? The key thing is to feel comfortable in giving your number out and not feeling rushed in giving your number and/or any other important information about yourself. Thus, once this information is given out, there is no going back. I do recognize we live in a world where text messaging is a way of life; however, once you're comfortable enough to exchange numbers, my strong suggestion is to actually use the number. To be clear, utilizing the number doesn't mean exchanges of text messages, but to physically talk on the phone and carry out conversations. Phone calls are very important because they usually allow individuals to get personal. Most people, even the shyest people, can talk "smack" in text messages but to actually talk on the phone with some allows you to truly be yourself. It also allows giving a person your full attention, and that's the way it should be, as you are trying to get to know someone. Phone conversations also allow you to pay attention to the sincerity in the other person's voice and to see if you can truly hold a conversation

Rule Number Six

Once you exchange phone numbers and you feel it's time to meet up, proceed with caution. I think in the world we live in today, we have truly forgotten what dating is. A first date should be at a public place and not take place at someone's home. Furthermore, a second and third date should not take place at a person's home either, whether you meet them online or in a public place. Even though having a date at someone's home may come across as cost-efficient and poses a comfortable setting, it is still a bad idea. By the first, second, and third date, how well do you truly know someone? Only you will know when the time is right to accept an invitation to someone—my advice is: take your time.

CHAPTER 7:

WHEN YOU'RE WILLING, I'M READY

O nce upon a time, it would have been difficult to expose the following information. But, in my personal journey, not only relationships but in addition to the ten (10) years working on this book, I've learned the importance of why this information needs to be shared. I've learned so much about love and relationships through my trials and errors – "recognizing what works in relationships and what doesn't." I understand the roles we play in break-ups and make ups. Recognizing strengths and weaknesses and how to apply them to benefit you in your relationship. But, it took me several years to understand, recognize, and accept the importance of what I will discuss in this chapter. When you're willing to sleep with me, I'll always be ready! We don't have to rush sex; we can take our time. I would not have uttered those words ten years ago, but with time comes growth and wisdom. I am not the same man I was ten (10) years ago, and I would hope none of my readers are either. How do you evolve as a person if your thought process on life doesn't change with the times? My mentality back then when it came to sex was: the quicker, the better. I felt that when you put time restraints on sex, it took away from the experience.

I knew whether you held off on sex, no matter the time frame, it wouldn't change a person's intent. If their intent is to sleep with you, that is all it will be, regardless of what barriers you put in place; There is one exception to this rule that I will discuss later on. However, when some men set out on that mission, they won't give up until it's accomplished. They may take a break, or even revisit the situation—hell, they may even disguise themselves as your friend, but in their mind, they are still plotting. You know the saying, ladies and gentlemen: "By Any Means Necessary." I mentioned there were exceptions. I took the liberty of listing some of the exceptions below.

1. Connection: Sex is not just a physical act, so it's amazing when you come across someone you feel heavily connected to. Have you ever kissed someone, touched someone, and you feel excited, at ease, fulfilled? I knew the first woman I fell in love with was like no other. When we kissed for the first time, it lasted for two hours. I felt at ease—I felt in my soul that she was someone special. When I met her, I wasn't looking for anything. I just thought she was so beautiful. But after we kissed, I knew I wanted more. I didn't want sex; I wanted *her.* I wanted to spend more time with her. I wanted to be her man and, eventually, her husband. I wanted to be whatever she needed me to be. Things were great for the time we

shared, but it didn't last. And even though it didn't last, which is not important, we remain friends to this day. My point is: some people will come in your life for the moment and others for a lifetime.

2. Sometimes when you have a strong feeling about something, you should explore it, even if that means exploring sex prematurely. We could have waited a little longer to have sex; however, it felt right. Have you ever met someone and felt so connected to them? You can spend time with someone and feel like you have known them forever. You can't put your finger on why, but it's a feeling you can't ignore. Well, in situations like that, only you can use your best judgment. But, even though the connection base can be a reason where a person's intention may change, if it's a true connection, it will play out naturally, and you won't have to rush anything.

I was such a free spirit back then when it came to love and sex, but my ideas have changed through my life experiences. Currently, I recognize sex as such a big responsibility. Sex has the ability to change the dynamic of a relationship. Sex is not just about the act but about making responsible choices, choices that can have positive and negative effects on a person's life. Once sex is involved, it can change the nature of a relationship. Before introducing sex to the relationship, you and your partner probably went out on dates a

36

lot. You guys might have had more insightful conversations. But in most cases, once sex is involved, those conversations may come to a screeching halt. Now that sex is involved, you're not dating as much. There may even be may long periods of silence on the phone when you two talk. If I hadn't said it already, conversation is very important when dating, and I don't mean texting. The most important conversations are the ones that happen in person so that you can truly "feel" a person out. Sometimes you can tell if a person is trying to bullshit you when you talk to them in person through their body language.

When dating, you should be making mental notes of the conversation you are having with a potential partner, and once you get comfortable enough, then you should consider introducing sex to the equation. If you introduce sex too early in the game, as I stated, things can change for the worse. At times, you might even find yourself accepting certain situations you wouldn't have normally accepted. You could be dating someone who told you they were single, and you find out later that they are involved with someone or even married, but their sex is so incredible that your desire for a relationship goes "out the window." So, it's crucial to maintain a clear mind as sex, especially great sex, can have you doing things outside of what you normally would do. It is so important in taking your time before having sex, as time reveals all. What I suggest in dating is: work on the friendship.

I'm not saying to place a person in the "friend zone," but take your time and make them earn your time. You can still be intimate without having sex, but recognize you are going down dangerous territories once intimacy is introduced in the dating factory. But forms of intimacy are what will separate things from being a total friendship. When I say: "total friendship," I'm referring to being placed in the friend zone. I'm also referring to phrases such as, "He's like my brother." However, with everything you do, you should always proceed with caution as we don't always know the consequences of our actions. So, keep in mind that when you're willing, when you have taken your time, truly feel comfortable, and have learned what you needed to learn about the person you are considering sleeping with, *then* you're ready.

CHAPTER 8:

THE PRETENDER

What often happens in dating is that we find ourselves meeting someone that appears to be ideal, but as time goes by, you learn they are nothing like the person you initially met. I advise everyone to avoid this person at all levels. The problem is that usually, these individuals are so good at pretending to be someone that they're not, hell, they are so good at pretending to be whoever they feel you want them to be that they fall right in between the cracks. Whether you are "playing it safe" or in the "right state of mind," there are ways that you can protect yourself from the pretender, ways I discussed in previous chapters. If you are fully aware of the situation and understand the dynamic of the dating game, that should allow you to see the red flags of the pretender. Overall, dating is truly about paying attention. When one pays attention to what a potential partner does and says, it equips you with knowledge. Knowledge is one of the most important things you can have in this world, and dating is no different.

If you feel the person who you are seeing is misleading you, just pay attention to what they say and what they do—time reveals all things. This is one of the reasons I spoke about taking your time before being intimate with someone, as time reveals all truths. If one is so quick to get involved with the fast-talking pretender, you can end up in an undesired situation. That is why it's important to take your time in dating someone because the number one thing most pretenders hate is patience. Being patient, observing, and listening will allow you to see anyone's true colors. Most pretenders hate this because you can't keep the charade going of being someone you aren't forever. Suppose you pay attention and ask enough questions, that person will slip, and their truth will reveal itself.

The most important thing you can do when meeting someone is truly paying attention to what they say *and* their habits. Later on, if they exhibit odd behavior or start doing things outside of their character, it will be somewhat of a red flag and more of a reason for you to investigate. As you get to know someone, you will realize whether or not they are truly genuine people—they will exhibit patterned behavior. It's only when they start acting out their perceived norm that causes room for alarm. You have some men who pretend they are single. However, most men are not single: they are usually involved in a relationship or have someone they are "involved" with on occasion. This normally complicates things, especially if that man isn't honest about his situation in the beginning. Most men feel when they are dating, they don't have to disclose certain information, considering that they don't know where things may lead with a person. You should always make it your business to know if there is possibly someone else in your potential partner's life, just for your own common knowledge. I believe women are usually single when entering new dating situations, only based on the mere fact that sex starts and ends with a woman giving permission for it to happen. With that being said, hold anyone accountable for what they tell you. When dating, hold that person accountable for their actions, especially when they get caught lying. Your standards for lying should be across the board. Most parents don't tolerate lying. In school, teachers don't tolerate lying. And most people in relationships shouldn't either. If you lie, you break trust.

In dating, you are trying to build trust, so if you break the trust in dating, there's no need for it to go any further to a relationship. Normally, everything about a pretender is a lie, so if you start to recognize suspicious behavior or things I mentioned in this chapter, don't be afraid to cut that person off. It's also important to be aware of individuals who are on a "come-up." Those are individuals who date with the intention of getting into a relationship for personal gain. This personal gain can vary but usually can be for the shelter you provide, as they may not have their own residence. It can also be for the wealth you have, as some people are naturally generous. Some people date individuals who they feel they can manipulate and get lavish gifts, trips, and money from. They date you intending to reap all the benefits you can provide.

1. ASK QUESTIONS: It's important to ask questions when dating. The only way you get the information you need is if you ask questions, as most people don't volunteer informa-

tion. If they do volunteer information, it's usually the only thing they want you to know. A suggestion would be to make a list of things you want to know about a person you are dating. This list can vary depending on the person but should consist of pertinent information: i.e., Personal information like their first and last name. Do they have children? Where do they work? Have they been arrested? When they give you this information, it's up to you to verify it. I know men who used to give women fake names and who used to lie about their residence. You can easily verify information in a playful way. You can ask a person to let you see their driver's license because you hate your license photo, and you have a feeling that their photo is so much better than yours. My point is, once you have your list, come up with clever ways to verify the information to ensure you are not dealing with a pretender.

2. PAY ATTENTION TO DETAIL: All people lie, but men lie about some of the dumbest things. One thing about a lie is it always comes out, so pay attention when you and your partner have conversations. Normally, when you think someone is lying, you're probably right. So, don't be afraid to revisit a flaky conversation a week later. I know I spoke about texting; however, this is a chance for you to use a text message against someone. You can have a conversation verbally about

something, then weeks later, revisit it with a text or do what I just suggested in reverse. If they are lying, now you have written proof. If you are only dating and they are lying to you, they should be cut off *immediately*. Your only responsibility when dating someone is really to be yourself and to be honest. If they can't do that while dating you, it won't get better if you are in a relationship or married.

3. PAY ATTENTION TO BEHAVIOR: It's always about playing it safe when dating. You want to see how a person you are dating handles anger. This anger doesn't have to be towards you but in general. They can have road rage or even be pissed off at a friend or family member. When they are angry, are they hitting objects or throwing things? If they have anger issues, you just want to ensure you will not be the person they take it out physically or mentally on—both can be forms of abuse.

4. HOLD THEM ACCOUNTABLE FOR WHEN THEY LIE: As I expressed, you must hold people accountable. Once you establish what type of person you want, and the person you are dating portrays themselves to be that person, you should only hold them accountable. If we start dating and I tell you that I want a relationship and you agree that you want the same thing, I'm going to assume nothing less. What happens on occasion is that you start dating someone, and months go

by, and you still are single on paper but unofficially in a relationship. Most men pretend to want to be in a relationship, so it's most important to let things be known in the dating process—let them know exactly what you want. So, if you feel after three months of dating that you should be in a relationship, then that should be known. If you feel after a year of dating, you and your mate should at least be discussing marriage, then that should be known as well. Men can only get away with what you allow and what you don't hold us accountable for. That's why it's so important to make your standards known. Fellas, women pretend too, so you should also be on the lookout, and the same rules apply. But, when it comes to dating and getting into relationships, men tend to play the *most* games.

THE PURPOSE

I t has been a long journey in writing this book, and I hope you were able to enjoy this book and learn some healthy tips that can assist you in moving forward in the dating process. I recognize that there may be individuals who may not agree with some of the material, and that's expected. But my goal was to raise awareness of the roles men and women play in dating and how it may affect potential relationships. I raised several points that I feel will be useful in the dating process, but I'll use these few points to conclude.

1. BE DIRECT: In dating, remember to always be direct with an individual with what you want and how you want it. Being direct ensures there isn't room for confusion in the dating process.

2. RECOGNIZE ALL RED FLAGS: A red flag can be as simple as a person lying about their age or marital status or what they may or may not do for a living. Simple red flags are always noticeable when you take your time and look. Don't always think with your heart.

3. BE TRUTHFUL: Being truthful is important in life and not limited to just dating. It's hard to keep up with lies that will

eventually see the light of day. One lie always leads to other lies, and a relationship must be built on trust, not lies.

4. ASK QUESTIONS: It's always important to ask questions. If you don't ask questions, how will you ever find out anything? Most people don't volunteer information. Most people won't volunteer the answers to the most important questions you may have. So, your job is to get the answers to the questions you feel are most important to you. Your questions can be answered, but how do you know if the information you are being told is the truth? You have to investigate.

5. INVESTIGATE: Trust has to be gained. If someone who you aren't that familiar with tried to sell you a dream, would you take it at face value? If someone tried to sell you a designer shirt for Walmart's prices and tries to pass it off as authentic, would you buy it, or would you investigate the authenticity? The point is that when you are starting a new relationship, you have to investigate things that sound too good to be true. I'm not telling you to stalk someone you are dating or break into their cell phone. But, I am saying that you should ask questions and maybe a few weeks later, have follow-up questions. It's hard to keep up with lies; they eventually catch up with a liar. This is also why I suggest taking your time before sleeping with someone as time reveals all.

6. BE OPEN TO CHANGE: Some people are so stuck in their ways. Don't be scared to venture into new territories. If things were going so great in your dating life, you wouldn't constantly be dating from one person to the next. It's important to understand that we, ourselves, have to take into account what type of people we are attracting and determine why we are attracting these people. We also need to understand when it comes to breakups and the struggle with dating that issues don't solely fall on individuals we are meeting, but it also may be our own doing.

7. EMBRACE YOUR INDEPENDENCE: This book was designed for women struggling with dating. However, most of the things that I've spoken about apply to both men and women as some men are struggling in finding the right mate. Embracing your independence is important, *especially* in the world that we live in today. It is expected for a man to be independent, especially when courting a woman. It's expecting men to be providers – provide safety and security in their relationship. However, women have evolved and, in most cases, are more independent than their male counterparts. Some women feel that their independence not only discourages men but makes them unattractive to men. If any man is discouraged or intimated by your independence, I can assure you they aren't strong enough to be with a woman like your-

self. Embrace your independence as it is a sign of strength, not weakness.

I would love for everyone who reads this book to use the information provided to their advantage. Most of this information lies in front of us, and we just ignore it. It usually takes one bad experience to make someone want to make a change. I hope with the information provided that you not only will make a change but that that change benefits in your dating experiences and helps you secure a healthy relationship.

FREQUENTLY ASKED QUESTIONS

When I took this journey in writing this book, I would be asked a variety of questions relating to love and relationships. Initially, I started to develop a blog to address these questions on a weekly basis through a question of a day section. However, as life happened, it proved to be tedious with my then work and personal schedule. For those who know me, know I've been working on this book for quite some time, and as a writer, not only do you want to make sure you get the best product out but that you take your time to ensure you get it to work to your overall vision. With that said, this section is solely dedicated to the most frequently asked questions I've been asked over the years.

WHY IS IT SO HARD FOR MEN TO EXPRESS THEIR FEELINGS?

AM: I PARTIALLY ANSWERED THIS QUESTION WHEN I WAS SPEAKING ABOUT HOW MEN AND WOMEN ARE TREATED SLIGHTLY DIFFERENT AS CHILDREN, UP UNTIL ADULTHOOD. DURING CHILDHOOD, BOYS ARE RAISED TO VIEW EMOTIONS AS A FORM OF WEAKNESS. MOST MOTHERS AND FATHERS TEACH THEIR SONS TO BE TOUGH AND ROUGH FROM AN EARLY AGE. THIS IS DONE

THROUGH THE SPORTS THEY PLAY TO HOW THEY HANDLE MOST SITUATIONS SUCH AS WHEN THEY FALL OFF A BIKE, HOW TO HANDLE BREAKUPS WITH A PARTNER, AND EVEN HOW TO HANDLE INTERACTIONS WITH PEOPLE. SHOWING AND EXPRESSING YOUR FEELINGS CAN BE VIEWED AS A FORM OF WEAKNESS AND VULNERABILITY. WHEN VULNERABLE AND WEAK, YOU COULD POSSIBLY FALL PREY TO MANIPULATION AND HEARTACHE. THIS IS WHY IT'S SO HARD FOR MOST MEN TO FALL IN LOVE. THUS FALLING IN LOVE WOULD BE FULLY EMBRACING ALL OF YOUR FEELINGS FOR SOMEONE AND ALLOWING YOURSELF TO POSSIBLY ENDURE A POTENTIAL HEARTACHE.

WHY ARE MEN AFRAID OF COMMITMENT?

AM: COMMITMENT CHANGES THE OUTLOOK OF A RELATIONSHIP. MOST MEN TECHNICALLY AREN'T AFRAID OF COMMITMENT, BUT RATHER THEY ARE NOT READY FOR COMMITMENT. WHEN YOU DO COMMIT TO SOMETHING, YOU ARE HELD TO A DIFFERENT STANDARD. THAT STANDARD CAN CHANGE THE WHOLE MAKE UP OF YOUR RELATIONSHIP. WHEN YOU COMMIT TO A PERSON, YOU ARE HELD MORE ACCOUNTABLE TOWARDS YOUR ACTIONS.

MOST MEN KNOW WHETHER THEY ARE READY FOR A COMMITMENT/RELATIONSHIP. A MAN WILL HAPPILY TELL YOU WHEN HE WANTS TO BE WITH YOU AND WHEN HE DESIRES MORE FROM A RELATIONSHIP WITH YOU. YOU WON'T HAVE TO FIGURE OUT WHAT PLACE YOU HOLD IN HIS LIFE IF HE TRULY WANTS TO BE WITH YOU. IF YOU HAVE TO ASK THE QUESTION, THAT MEANS HE IS NOT READY TO COMMIT. IF HE'S NOT READY TO COMMIT, HE WILL HAVE YOU IN A SITUATIONSHIP. HE WILL HAVE YOU TAKING ON THE DUTIES AS IF YOU WERE IN A MONOGA-MOUS RELATIONSHIP. JUST BECAUSE A PERSON HAS YOU IN A SITUATIONSHIP DOESN'T MEAN THEY DON'T WANT TO BE IN A COMMITtED RELATIONSHIP WITH YOU. IN MOST CASES, THEY AREN'T READY TO BE HELD AC-COUNTABLE FOR THE GUIDELINES A FULLY COMMITtED RELATIONSHIP ENTAILS

IS IT OK FOR A WOMAN TO PURSUE A MAN OR PROPO-SE MARRIAGE TO A MAN?

AM: WE LIVE IN DIFFERENT TIMES FROM WHEN OUR PARENTS AND GRANDPARENTS WERE COMING UP. MORALS ARE DIFFERENT; EVERYDAY LIFE IS DIFFERENT. I WAS RAISED WITH THE BELIEF THAT A MAN SHOULD

PURSUE A WOMAN, TO BE A PROVIDER. HOWEVER, WE LIVE IN A SOCIETY WHERE YOU NEED TWO INCOMES. WE LIVE IN A SOCIETY WHERE WOMAN ARE CARING FOR OUR CHILDREN, TAKING CARE OF A MANS EVERY NEED, AND WORKING A FULL-TIME JOB TO CONTRIBUTE TO THE HOUSEHOLD. SO WOMEN ARE DOING ALL OF THESE THINGS I MENTIONED WHILE SOME OF US MEN HAVE ONE JOB AND CANNOT COOK. ALL OF THAT BEING SAID, I DON'T THINK A WOMAN SHOULD PURSUE A MAN. IF A MAN WANTS TO MARRY YOU, HE WILL PROPOSE. A MAN ALREADY KNOWS FROM THE MOMENT HE MAKES THE COMMITMENT OF BEING IN A RELATIONSHIP WITH YOU, WHICH DIRECTION HE WANTS THE RELATIONSHIP TO GO. IT DOESN'T TAKE 2-5 YEARS TO FIGURE OUT WHETHER HE WANTS TO SPEND THE REST OF HIS LIFE WITH YOU, AND IF IT HAS, THEN HE MAY BE PROPOSING OUT OF OBLIGATION AND NOT BECAUSE HE'S TRULY IN LOVE WITH YOU. DON'T GET ME WRONG, SOME MEN WANT TO GET THEMSELVES TOGETHER TO BE IN A PLACE WHERE THEY CAN TRULY PROVIDE. A REAL MAN KNOWS THE IMPORTANCE OF BEING A PROVIDER FOR THEMSELVES AS WELL AS FOR THEIR FAMILY, BUT I STILL FEEL THAT IS AN EXCUSE, BECAUSE IF YOU ARE TRULY WHO THEY WANT TO BE WITH, PROPOSING WON'T GET IN THE WAY

OF THAT. IT MAY BE MORE OF A MOTIVATIONAL TOOL FOR THEM, TO GRIND HARDER. PLAIN AND SIMPLE, WOMEN SHOULD PURSUE MEN. I DO THINK A WOMAN CAN GIVE SUBLIMINAL MESSAGES TO A MAN THAT YOU ARE INTERESTED. YOU CAN GIVE A MAN YOUR NUMBER. BUT MEN ARE NATURAL HUNTERS. SOME OF US MEN ARE SHY AND MAY NEED A LITTLE ASSISTANCE IN PURSING YOU. BUT BY GIVING CERTAIN MESSAGES THAT YOU ARE INTERESTED IN BEING PURSUED GOES ALONG WAY.

IS IT ACCEPTABLE FOR A MAN TO SEE YOU ONCE A WEEK?

AM: NO! MARRIED MEN MAKE TIME FOR AFFAIRS, SO IT'S UNACCEPTABLE FOR SOMEONE WHO IS SUPPOSE TO BE SINGLE TO SEE YOU ONCE A WEEK. THERE ARE THREE REAL REASONS WHY A MAN MAY SEE YOU ONCE A WEEK.

1. HE'S MARRIED OR INVOLVED! WHEN YOU ARE MARRIED DEPENDING ON THE NATURE OF YOUR MARRIAGE, YOUR TIME MAY BE LIMITED, SO YOU MAY ONLY HAVE TIME TO SEE SOMEONE WHEN TIME PERMITS. HOWEVER, A MARRIED MAN CAN HAVE SUCH A STRONG RELATIONSHIP WITH THE OTHER WOMAN THAT HE MAKES IT HIS BUSINESS TO SEE THIS WOMAN WHENEVER HE HAS ANY EX-

TRA TIME FAR EXCEEDING ONCE A WEEK. IF A MARRIED MAN CAN DO IT. IT SHOULD COME EASIER FOR A SINGLE MAN. YOUR TIME WITHIN YOUR MARRIAGE MAY BE MONITORED BY YOUR PARTNER, SO IT MAY BE A LITTLE HARDER, BUT IF YOU'RE REALLY INTO THE OTHER WOMAN, THERE IS NO COST THAT YOU WOULD NOT INCUR TO SEE THE OTHER WOMAN. IF YOU HAVE CHILDREN TOGETHER, WHATEVER FREE TIME YOU HAVE MAY BE DEVOTED TO THE CHILDREN AND FAMILY LIFE. IF YOU ARE SINGLE AND HAVE CHILDREN, YOU HAVE A LITTLE MORE FREEDOM THEN IF YOU ARE INVOLVED WITH THE MOTHER OF YOUR CHILDREN. HOWEVER, IF HE'S REALLY INTO YOU, HE WILL FIND A WAY TO SEE YOU MORE THAN ONCE, ESPECIALLY IF YOU COMPLAIN.

2. DISTANCE! DEPENDING ON EACH OF YOUR LIVING LOCATIONS, IT CAN BE A STRENUOUS COMMUTE, OR YOU CAN BE IN DIFFERENT STATES. IF THAT IS THE CASE, THEN HE MAY BE INTO YOU, BUT THE DISTANCE IS TRULY THE ISSUE, NOT HIS FEELINGS. LONG DISTANCE RELATIONSHIP TAKE A LITTLE MORE PATIENCE AND UNDERSTANDING. A LONG DISTANCE RELATIONSHIP WOULD BE THE ONLY

CASE WHERE IT'S ACCEPTABLE TO SEE EACH OTH-ER ONCE A WEEK, ESPECIALLY DEPENDING ON HOW FAR THE DISTANCE IS.

3. HE'S JUST NOT INTO YOU! HE MAY LIKE BEING IN-TIMATE WITH YOU BUT NOT BE FULLY INTO YOU. HE MAY DEAL WITH YOU ON A WEEK-TO-WEEK BASIS TO ENSURE HE DOESN'T CATCH FEELINGS AND TO AVOID GETTING CAUGHT IF HE'S INDEED INVOLVED AND/OR MARRIED.

WHY WOULD A MARRIED MAN/WOMAN PROFESS HIS/ HER LOVE TO ANOTHER?

AM: DO YOU BELIEVE YOU CAN LOVE MORE THEN ONE PERSON? IT'S DIFFICULT TO HIDE FEELINGS THAT AL-READY EXIST. IN A LOT OF CASES WHEN MARRIED INDI-VIDUALS PROFESS THEIR LOVE TO ANOTHER, IT'S DUE TO THEM HAVING A RELATIONSHIP, UNLIKE THE ONE THEY SHARE WITH THEIR PARTNER. MOST MARRIED MEN & WOMAN WILL NOT CHEAT JUST TO GET THE SAME FEELING OR THRILLS THEY CAN RECEIVE FROM THEIR PARTNER. SO WHEN A MAN & WOMAN PROFESS THEIR

LOVE NINETY PERCENT OF THE TIME, IT'S CONNECTION BASED. A LOT OF MARRIED PEOPLE ARE NOT MARRIED DUE TO BEING IN LOVE WITH EACH OTHER. MOST OF THE TIME, IT'S OBLIGATION, LOYALTY, FINANCIAL GAIN, AND COMPANIONSHIP. THAT BEING SAID, A MARRIED INDIVIDUAL CAN LOVE THEIR PARTNER BUT HAVE A DEEPER CONNECTION WITH SOMEONE ELSE. THE NEXT QUESTION SHOULD BE, WHY NOT BE WITH THE OTHER PERSON? WELL, LIFE, LOVE, AND RELATIONSHIPS ARE NEVER EASY. SOMETIMES YOU CAN LOVE SOMEONE SO MUCH, BUT THAT PERSON NOT BE THE RIGHT FIT FOR YOU. HAVE YOU EVER BEEN WITH SOMEONE AND THINGS ARE GREAT. YOU CAN TALK ABOUT ANY AND EVERYTHING. WHEN YOU'RE INTIMATE, IT'S AMAZING. BUT FOR SOME REASON WHEN YOU GUYS ARGUE, YOU CAN GO DAYS, EVEN WEEKS WITHOUT SPEAKING TO ONE ANOTHER. YOU HAVE A DEEP BOND, OF COURSE, BECAUSE WHEN YOU GUYS FIND YOUR WAY BACK TO ONE ANOTHER, IT'S GREAT, BUT IT ONLY LAST LONG ENOUGH TO THE NEXT ARGUMENT. YOU MAY DEEPLY LOVE THAT PERSON, BUT IT'S STILL AN UNHEALTHY RELATIONSHIP BECAUSE NO MATTER HOW ANGRY YOU ARE WITH SOMEONE YOU LOVE, YOU SHOULDN'T BE ABLE TO GO A WEEK, EVEN A FEW DAYS WITHOUT SPEAKING TO THEM. MY POINT IS

THAT NOT EVERYONE WHO'S MARRIED HAVE THOSE
FEELINGS FOR THEIR PARTNER. SOMETIMES YOU CAN'T
BE WITH WHO YOU FEEL YOUR HEART TRULY BELONGS
TO, AND IN THAT EVENT, YOU MOVE FORWARD.

DO YOU NEED A PARTNER TO FEEL WHOLE/COMPLE-TE?

AM: YOU SHOULD NEVER FEEL THAT YOU NEED A COM-PANION TO FEEL COMPLETE. AND IF YOU FELT OR FEEL
THAT WAY, THAT MAY BE A STRONG REASON WHY YOU
ARE SINGLE AND STILL SEARCHING. IF YOU LOOKING
FOR A RELATIONSHIP TO FEEL COMPLETE, WHAT HAP-PENS WHEN THAT RELATIONSHIP IS BROKEN & OVER. I
MENTIONED IN ONE OF MY CHAPTERS THAT YOU NEED
TO RECOGNIZE YOUR STRENGTHS AND WEAKNESSES. IN
ORDER FOR YOU TO TRY TO PLEASE SOMEONE AND
MAKE SOMEONE HAPPY, YOU WOULD TRULY NEED TO
KNOW WHAT MAKES YOU HAPPY. YOU NEED TO HAVE A
SENSE OF SELF BEFORE YOU CAN TAKE ON A PROJECT OF
ANOTHER PERSON. ANY PERSON YOU ALLOW IN YOUR
LIFE SHOULD BE AN ADDED BONUS. YOU ARE THE FULL
PACKAGE ALWAYS, AND YOU DON'T NEED A RELATION-SHIP TO VALIDATE YOU.

WHAT HAPPENS IS WHEN A PERSON IS NOT A WHOLE, THEY YERN FOR COMPANIONSHIP DUE TO LONELINESS AND THE SENSE OF SECURITY. THE SAD PART OF THAT IS YOU MAY FALL FOR ANYTHING AND ANYONE COMPROMISING YOUR STANDARDS AND SETTLING FOR WHAT COMES YOUR WAY JUST TO HAVE A PARTNER. AND IN MOST CASES, THOSE SITUATIONS ARE TEMPORARY FIXES TO A LARGER PROBLEM. ALL IN ALL, YOU DON'T NEED A PARTNER TO COMPLETE YOU. WORK ON YOURSELF, EMPOWER YOURSELF AND LEARN ABOUT YOURSELF. HOW WELL DO YOU KNOW YOURSELF, THE THINGS YOU LIKE AND DISLIKE? DATING IS ONEWAY TO LEARN ABOUT THESE THINGS, BUT WHY NOT DATE YOURSELF? TAKE YOURSELF OUT, TREAT YOURSELF. NO ONE CAN TAKE BETTER CARE OF YOU THAN YOU. THAT'S WHAT I MEAN BY EMPOWER YOURSELF. ONCE YOU EMPOWER YOURSELF, EVERYTHING ELSE WILL FALL RIGHT IN PLACE.

SHOULD YOU EVER GIVE UP WANTING TO BE IN A RELATIONSHIP AFTER BEING IN NUMEROUS FAILED RELATIONSHIPS? HOW CAN YOU TURN THINGS AROUND?

AM: I PERSONALLY DON'T BELIEVE IN GIVING UP. FOR EVERY FAILED ATTEMPT AT SOMETHING YOU STRIVED TO GET. THERE IS ALWAYS A LESSON TO BE LEARNED. FOR EVERY BAD DATING EXPERIENCE, YOU SHOULD BE ABLE

TO TAKE SOMETHING GOOD AND BAD FROM IT. THE BAD THINGS YOU SHOULD BE ABLE TO UTILIZE IN YOUR NEXT DATING EXPERIENCE AS SOMETHING TO AVOID. YOU SHOULD ALSO LOOK AT YOUR DATING BEHAVIOR, RECOGNIZE SOME OF YOUR STRENGTHS AND WEAKNESS AND APPLY THEM GOING FORWARD. A LOT OF INDIVIDUALS FAIL TO CHANGE THEIR DATING BEHAVIOR OR EVEN ACKNOWLEDGE SOME OF THEIR OWN PROBLEMS WHEN DATING. THIS USUALLY RESULTS IN THEM DATING THE SAME TYPE OF PEOPLE. WHEN I SPEAK TO MEN AND WOMEN, I ALWAYS ASK, HOW DID YOUR LAST RELATIONSHIP END? AND MOST PEOPLE USUALLY PLACE BLAME ON THE PARTNER. I THEN ASK WHAT ROLE DID YOU PLAY IN THE BREAKUP. AS WE ALL PLAY A PART IN WHY THINGS END IN A RELATIONSHIP. RELATIONSHIP INVOLVES TWO PEOPLE, AND EVEN THOUGH ONE PERSON CAN BE A MAJOR REASON WHY A BREAKUP HAPPENS, ITS ONLY LOGIC TO DETERMINE WHAT ROLE YOU PLAYED. EVEN WHEN A PERSON CHEATS OR THERE ARE FINANCIAL ISSUES IN RELATIONSHIPS, EVEN THOUGH YOU WEREN'T THE ONE WITH THE DIRECT PROBLEM, WHAT DID YOU DO TO SOLVE IT. WHEN YOU'RE IN A RELATIONSHIP, YOU'RE ACTUALLY ON A TEAM, SO WHEN ONE TEAMMATE SUFFERS, THE TEAM SUFFERS.

IN ORDER TO TURN A FAILED RELATIONSHIP TO A GOOD ONE, YOU NEED TO FIRST RECOGNIZE YOUR STRENGTHS AND ACKNOWLEDGE YOUR WEAKNESSES. THE IDEA COMES FROM THE FACT THAT NO ONE IS PERFECT. SOMETIMES OUR BIGGEST STRENGTH CAN BE A WEAKNESS, AND WEAKNESS CAN BE A STRENGTH. I DISCUSSED THE IMPORTANCE OF EMPOWERING YOURSELF AND KNOWING YOURSELF IN THE LAST QUESTION ANSWERED. IF YOU UTILIZE THIS IN YOUR DATING BEHAVIOR, YOU MAY SEE THINGS CLEARLY. SO CLEAR THAT YOU WILL BE ABLE TO AVOID GETTING INTO TOXIC RELATIONSHIPS. THE POINT IS, ONCE YOU RECOGNIZE WHO YOU ARE AS A PERSON AND WHAT YOU WANT AND NEED FROM A RELATIONSHIP, THE DATING PROCESS WILL COME EASIER. WHEN THE DATING PROCESS COMES EASIER, IT MAKES IT EASIER TO ALIGN YOURSELF WITH SOMEONE WHO NOT ONLY FITS YOUR CRITERIA BUT IS YOUR CRITERIA. THAT'S WHY YOU SHOULD NEVER GIVE UP AFTER ANY FAILED RELATIONSHIP ATTEMPTS, AND THAT'S HOW YOU TURN THINGS AROUND.

HOW CAN YOU LOVE AND PROTECT YOUR HEART AT THE SAME TIME?

AM: HONESTLY, YOU CAN'T! HOW CAN YOU TRULY LOVE OR FALL IN LOVE WITH SOMEONE WHEN YOUR LOVE

COMES WITH LIMITATIONS. WHEN YOU PROTECT YOUR-
SELF USUALLY, YOU SHIELD YOURSELF FROM POTEN-
TIAL HURT. YOU MAY NOT LOOK AT IT LIKE THAT, BUT
WHEN YOU HURT, IT MAKES YOU STRONGER. I CAN
COUNT ON MY FINGERS ON EVERY TIME I WAS HURT AND
A FEW MONTHS AFTER, I MET SOMEONE BETTER THAN
THE PREVIOUS PREDECESSOR. WITH HURT COMES
GROWTH, WHAT COMES WITH GROWTH IS WISDOM. YOU
CAN LOVE SMARTER. YOU CAN MAKE BETTER DECI-
SIONS WHEN DATING. AS I OUTLINED IN THE BOOK, MAK-
ING BETTER DECISION IS ALL ABOUT PAYING ATTENTION
TO A POTENTIAL PARTNER. PLAYING IT SAFE WHEN DAT-
ING BY AVOIDING GETTING TO A SITUATION OR AC-
KNOWLEDGING A PRETENDER FROM A MILE AWAY. AND
LASTLY, BEING IN THE RIGHT STATE OF MIND, KNOWING
WHO YOU ARE, WHAT YOU WANT, AND HOW YOU WANT
IT. WHEN YOU KNOW THESE THINGS, YOU FIND YOUR-
SELF NOT SETTLING, NOT COMPROMISING, BUT BEING
VERY DIRECT WITH WHOEVER YOU DECIDE TO ALLOW IN
YOUR LIFE. AND THAT DOES A BIG PART OF THE JOB BE-
CAUSE IT ELIMINATES INDIVIDUALS WHO TRULY DON'T
HAVE YOUR BEST INTENTIONS. YOU MAY NOT BE ABLE
TO PROTECT YOUR HEART, BUT YOU CAN DEFINITELY
LOVE SMARTER.

WHY WOULD A MAN BE INTIMIDATED BY A WOMAN?

AM: THERE ARE NORMALLY TWO REASONS MEN ARE USUALLY INTIMATED BY WOMEN. ONE REASON IS DUE TO THEIR OWN INSECURITIES. REAL MEN ARE DEFINED BY THE SECURITY THEY CAN PROVIDE, WHICH IS NOT LIMITED TO SHELTER, PROTECTION, AND THE ABILITY TO LEAD THEIR HOUSEHOLD. A MAN WHO'S COMFORTABLE WITH HIMSELF AND POSITION IN LIFE WOULD NOT BE INTIMIDATED. BUT A MAN WHO'S STILL FINDING HIS WAY WOULD. WHAT CAN YOU OFFER SOMEONE WHO APPEARS SELF- SUFFICIENT? IF YOU ARE TRULY SECURE WITHIN YOURSELF, YOU ACKNOWLEDGING A STRONG WOMAN ONLY MAKES A POTENTIAL RELATIONSHIP MORE AP-PEALING. A MAN NEEDS TO BUILD HIMSELF UP AND FIND NICHE, LEARN HIS PURPOSE BEFORE HE EVEN TRYS TO PURSUE YOU. I'LL SPEAK MORE ABOUT THIS IN MY NEXT BOOK IN A CHAPTER CALLED THE PROJECT. AS A WOMAN, BEWARE OF TAKING ON BROKEN MEN, MEN THAT ARE STILL FINDING THEIR WAY. MEN & WOMEN TAKE YOUR TME TO LEARN WHAT IT IS YOU WANT AND DETERMINE WHAT YOU NEED FROM DATING. ACKNOWL-EDGED ONCE YOU HAVE THESE THINGS, WHAT CONTRI-BUTION CAN YOU MAKE TO THIS POSSIBLE RELATION-

SHIP? ASK YOURSELF, ARE YOU EVEN READY TO BE IN A RELATIONSHIP? ARE YOU HAPPY AND SECURE WITH YOURSELF? HAVE YOU REACHED A GOAL OF HAPPINESS WITHIN YOURSELF? THE REAL QUESTION IS HOW CAN YOU STRIVE TO MAKE SOMEONE HAPPY IN A RELATION-SHIP WHEN YOU AREN'T HAPPY WITHIN YOURSELF. A LOT OF MAN AREN'T HAPPY WITHIN THEMSELVES OR KNOW WHAT MAKES THEM TRULY HAPPY, AND THAT IS WHAT BRINGS ON INSECURITIES.

AM: THE SECOND REASON CAN BE THE FACT THAT YOU'RE AN IDEAL FOR HIM. MOST MEN WANT A TROPHY WIFE. EVERY MAN'S TROPHY WIFE WILL VARY DEPEND-ING ON THEIR PREFERENCES. FOR THE MOST PART, A TROPHY WIFE WOULD BE THE MOST BEAUTIFUL WOMAN THEY HAVE LAID EYES ON WITH THE MOST AMAZING FIGURE. THAT WOMAN MAY COOK LIKE SHE'S A CHEF AND SEX LIKE A GODDESS. THE ONLY PROBLEM FOR MOST MEN IS WHETHER THEY ARE YOU WORTHY OF SUCH A WOMAN. A MAN CAN BE INTIMIDATED BECAUSE HE'S LOOKING AT WHAT HE FEELS IS HIS IDEAL AND SIKE HIMSELF OUT. HE MAY FEEL THIS WOMAN HIS OUT OF HIS LEAGUE BASED UPON HIS OWN PERCEPTION. WHAT NEEDS TO BE UNDERSTOOD IS THAT THERE ISNT ANY-THING YOU CAN OR SHOULD DO ABOUT THIS. WHAT I

EXPLAIN TO A LOT OF WOMEN THAT I ENCOUNTER IS THAT FINDING THE RIGHT PARTNER TAKES TIME. STAY TRUE TO YOURSELF AND WHAT YOU WANT, AND THE RIGHT PERSON WHO WAS CREATED JUST FOR YOU WILL COME. YOU SHOULDN'T HAVE TO COMPROMISE OR SETTLE IN THE PROCESS.

WHY DO MEN LIE ABOUT THEIR RELATIONSHIP STATUS?

AM: MEN CAN BE VERY SELFISH AND TERRITORIAL. WE WANT WHAT WE WANT AND THAT AT TIMES COMES AT THE EXPENSE OF BEING TRUTHFUL TO A PERSON WE ARE INVOLVE WITH OR POTENTIALLY WOULD LIKE TO BE INVOLVED WITH. MEN WOULD BE MORE TRUTHFUL IF THEY FELT IT WOULD ENSURE THEY WOULD BE ABLE TO GET WHAT THEY WANT. MEN OFTEN PORTRAY TO BE SOMEONE THEY AREN'T UST TO GET WHAT THEY WANT. I SPOKE ABOUT THIS IN CHAPTER SIX, "THE PRETENDER." MEN HAVE A HABIT OF GIVING HALF TRUTHS, WHICH IS NEVER RIGHT. BECAUSE OF THIS, WHEN MEETING A WOMAN, A MAN HAS A CHOICE, TO BE HONEST, OR TO LIE. MOST MEN BASE HOW MUCH TRUTH THEY WILL TELL YOU UPON THEIR PERCEPTION OF YOU, AND BY THE

CONVERSATIONS YOU HAVE. A MARRIED OR INVOLVED MAN MAY NOT TELL YOU THEIR SITUATION RIGHT AWAY. THEY MAY TELL YOU THEY ARE INVOLVED OR DOWN-PLAY THE SITUATION. THEY MAY TELL YOU THEY ARE SINGLE BUT DATING. BY TELLING YOU THEY ARE DAT-ING, THEY ARE LETTING YOU KNOW THERE IS POSSIBLY SOMEONE ELSE. BY LETTING YOU KNOW THEY ARE IN-VOLVED, THEY ARE TELLING YOU A SMALL TRUTH. SO IF YOU DO DECIDE TO GET INVOLVE AND YOU GUYS ARE INTIMATE, IT MAKES IT EASIER TO SHARE THE FULL TRUTH THEN, BECAUSE SEX USUALLY CHANGE THE DY-NAMIC OF THE RELATIONSHIP. THAT'S WHY I'VE SUG-GESTED IN THIS BOOK TO TAKE YOUR TIME BEFORE BE-COMING INTIMATE WITH SOMEONE AND LET THINGS RE-VEAL ITSELF.

WHEN SHOULD YOU TELL A MAN YOU LOVE THEM WITHOUT SCARING THEM OFF?

AM: THERE IS NEVER A RIGHT TIME TO TELL SOMEONE YOU LOVE THEM. AND ITS VERY DIFFICULT IN DETER-MINING IF SOMEONE LOVES YOU. THERE ISN'T A RIGHT OR WRONG WAY IN EXPRESSING YOUR LOVE, ESPECIAL-LY WHEN YOU UNDERSTAND THAT WE ALL LOVE DIF-FERENTLY. SOME PEOPLE SHOW THEIR LOVE BY PUR-

CHASING GIFTS FOR A LOVED ONE, OTHERS SHOW THEIR LOVE VERBALLY OR THROUGH THEIR ACTIONS. NO ONE LIKES REJECTION SO THE REAL ISSUE ISN'T ABOUT SCARING THE PERSON OFF BUT RATHER THE PERSON REJECTING YOU. DEVELOPING LOVE FOR SOMEONE HAPPENS NATURALLY. SO, YOU SHOULD NEVER CONCERN YOURSELF WITH SCARING SOMEONE OFF BY EXPRESSING THE LOVE YOU HAVE FOR THEM. IN MOST CASES IF YOU FEEL THAT YOU WOULD SCARE THE PERSON OFF, IN MY OPINION THEY PROBABLY ARENT THE BEST CHOICE FOR YOU. SUBCONSCIOUSLY I BELIEVE WE KNOW WHAT SITUATIONS ARE GOOD FOR US AND WHAT ARE BAD. SO IF YOU THINK YOU WOULD SCARE THE PERSON OFF ITS PROBABLY BECAUSE YOU ALREADY KNOW THAT THE PERSON ISNT REALLY INTO YOU

"CHEAT" NOTES

www.ingramcontent.com/pod-product-compliance
Lightning Source LLC
Chambersburg PA
CBHW072213270326
41930CB00011B/2622